Simone Weil: Songs of Hunger and Love

Simone Weil: Songs of Hunger and Love

Sarah Klassen

Wolsak and Wynn . Toronto

© Sarah Klassen, 1999

All rights reserved. No part of this book may be reproduced or transmitted in any form, by any means, electronic or mechanical, without permission in writing from the publisher, except by a reviewer who may quote brief passages in a review. In case of photocopying or other reprographic copying, a licence is required from CANCOPY (Canadian Copyright Licensing Agency), One Yonge Street, Suite 1900, Toronto, ON, CANADA M5E 1E5.

Typeset in Galliard, printed in Canada by
The Coach House Printing Company, Toronto.

Cover image: ©Helen Dyck

Author's photograph: Larry J. Mahler

Poems in this collection have appeared, sometimes in a slightly different form, in the following publications: *Canadian Forum, Event, The Fiddlehead, The New Quarterly, The NeWest Review, Prairie Fire.*

The publishers are grateful to the Canada Council for the Arts and the Ontario Arts Council. for supporting our publishing program.

Wolsak and Wynn Publishers Ltd.
Post Office Box 316
Don Mills, Ontario
Canada M3C 2S7

Canadian Cataloguing in Publication Data

Klassen, Sarah, 1932-
    Simone Weil: songs of hunger and love

ISBN 0-919897-65-7

1. Weil, Simone, 1909-1943 – Poetry. I. Title.

PS8571.L386S55 1999   C811'.54   C99-930858-0
PR9199.3.K468S55 1999

2nd Printing

Contents

I. Hunger

Beginning   11
Hunger I   12
At the piano   13
Eiffel Tower   14
A reading list   15
Childhood   16
Adolescence   17
Idealist   18
Hunger II   19
Lyrics from a *lycée*   20
Character   24
Pensées   25

II. God exists because I desire him

How to become anonymous   29
Defence   30
On vacation   32
Making the rate (factory journals)   33
Pilgrims of the absolute   38
Credo   39
Jew   41
Sanctuary   43
In Paris   44
Revolution   45
Interlude   46
Stations   47
Baptism   50
Pensées   51

III. We can only cry out

Places of abandonment   55
Letters to Antonio, 1940   58
Exile   63
Memos to a government in exile   66
Pensées   68
Colour   70
Centre   71
London, 1943   72
Letter to a friend   73
Morning   74
Love song   75
Still hungry   76
Grief   77
Room   78
Outside the gate   79
Dirge   80

We must only wait and call out. Not call upon someone, while we still do not know if there is anyone; but cry out that we are hungry and want bread. Whether we cry for a long time or a short time, in the end we shall be fed, and then we shall *know* that there really is bread. What surer proof could one ask for than to have eaten it?
— *Simone Weil*

Blessed are those who hunger and thirst for righteousness, for they will be filled.
— *Matthew 5:6*

Love is not consolation, it is light.
— *Simone Weil*

There is no great genius without some touch of madness.
— *Seneca*

I. HUNGER

Beginning

In the beginning the world bursts open
a shimmering opal. In the Luxembourg Gardens
birds carol, an iridescent twittering of joy.
The dew-wet morning grass moves like the sea.

Nights those reticent pin-point stars appear
neither cold nor distant. (What do I know
of distance?)
                I touch them

with my new-born fingertips, trace the diamond
rhythm of their music. Proof enough
(I am sure those fervent days) of truth.
I have no need for words that promise love. No need

for further evidence. The madly spinning
and expanding universe
holds for one fragile moment
only light.

Hunger I

I was born hungry.
Nothing in the whole world would ever be enough.
Daybreak to dusk my small mouth gaping
like a bird's for food.
It wasn't mother-milk, her warm breasts given
gladly, my father's need to make things better
I desired.

    Only blue sky, the stunning depth of it,
a sudden harmony of curved light, an organ chord
could prune the sharpest edge off
my wanting. How should they have known,
my mother, my kind father:
their joined flesh, satisfied,
could generate voraciousness,
spawn such unseemly thirst and this
unearthly appetite.

At the piano

Grandmother at the piano
gentle as faded lace, white hair a gracious halo
in the lamplight, fingers raised mid-melody.
Russia drifts adagio through her mind tonight:
dazzling crescendos of silk
swelling from overstuffed chairs.
Steaming samovar,
gold and silver vessels the footman fills
with caviar and wine. How long

I wonder can she hold her slender hands
poised, pale featherless birds
hanging in air,
their wings a curved cadence.
How long till they crash down in dissonant rage,
the splintered notes flung terrified along the keyboard,
across the years. They ricochet like bullets from the jewels
concealed in corsets of the Empress in the impeccable
garments of her daughters.

Nothing the fingers can do to blunt the hard theme's edge:
Bayonets brutal as thorns thrust
deep into virgin flesh that's faultless,
warm as any turtledove's.
And terrified.

Eiffel Tower

Cradled in my mother's arms
I'm carried, a small sacrifice, to the operating room,
holding tight to promises she makes:
true light
transforming a green tree
making it glow with stars the moment I arrive.

Struggling against the cold stranglehold of ether
I can no longer face doctors
not even my father. Can never look up
without terror towering dark inside me.

Black against the blinding sky
the cruel Eiffel Tower
crowds out the healing sun on my way
to the hospital
cradled warmly in my mother's arms.

A reading list

My parents permitted me to share my crib
with a pink book. Stories by Larousse
instructed me in cruelty of Rome.
When I stood upright in my bed
proclaiming *I'm afraid
of the Romans*
my parents were amused.

Refusing food I consumed tragedy
and comedy,
Karl Marx, Descartes.
The lives of Seneca, Prometheus
pulsed through my blood.
I sampled Sanskrit and Greek
tasted the *Bhagavad-Gita* and became
sated with Babylonian. I craved Dante's
poetry, claimed Gilgamesh for mine.

The Hebrew scriptures brutishly reminded me
of Rome, for which I had no stomach
as I've said. The words of Lear defined affliction
bitterly inside me. I became a glutton:
Swallowed the Iliad whole
devoured the best of Plato
and hoarded the hard gospel
stories in my heart.

Childhood

My brother taught me when I was six to read the newspaper as a present for Papa, a doctor, and to recite Racine. We refused patriotically to eat chocolate and sugar, sending them instead to soldiers fighting valiantly for France. I believed all the children in the world played as we did, brother and sister in chorus chanting math formulas, preferring the brilliant splash of an autumn sunset on the ocean to games. At ten I fashioned a fairy tale about sylphs, the brightly robed souls of unborn children. The tale was mystery, the ending moral as I could make it.

At fourteen, convinced of my mediocrity, I prepared to die. What use in living except for the brilliant like my brother whom I loved. Only those blest as he is have the hope of entering the glad kingdom of truth, the only kingdom I yearned for. It was more desirable to me than salvation or promises of love. To be shut out forever from its perfect clarity would be unbearable.

Adolescence

I did not care to inhabit entirely my childlike body which I despised for its frailty and complete absence of grace. *Why don't you comb your hair* they said. *Pay more attention to the style and colour of your clothes.* But I lived mainly in my head where I was most at home. Where I considered in the brain's free convolutions the brute force of necessity, learned the torment of attending to an absolute truth not yet defined although its thin edge grew and grew until it tore cruelly at my heart.

About this time the headaches started, their bludgeoning proved more faithful than friends. I became half-blind, an intermittent cripple, groping through pain that pounded with the force of hoof beats in my head. It outshouted my words, outgrew my feet, my small awkward hands. They noticed none of this, diverted by the turbulent shock of my hair, my spectacles' thick lenses and the poor fit of my overcoat.

Idealist

I was desperate to eat at the plain table of the poor
drink the wine of hard labour.
Hunger and thirst drove me in summer
to a farm family who permitted me to live
simply, draw water for the cows
heap up manure with my thin arms
unearth obstinate beetroot.

They offered me black coffee
cream cheese which I refused
craving frugality and bare truth.
When I enquired of their desires, they did not speak
about the earth's abundant beauty, rain
clinging to grape leaves
the moon's translucence.
No one mentioned contentment.

The silence spread a heaviness between us.
I spoke of bloodshed we'd have to endure
in order to overleap the pity
naked in their eyes. At last I realized
my hands were unwashed from the fields
my clothes unclean
my hunger a millstone so immense
no one would beg me to stay.

Hunger II

They kept telling me to eat,
eat this bread, fragrant and freshly buttered
these fine herrings, a handful of purple grapes.
Drink more milk they said
and try this well-aged wine.
Chewing was too much and nothing
would go down right.

When I settled for cigarettes they complained:
burns on the table cloth
ashes scattered carelessly. Besides
my clumsy fingers fumbled
rolling the cigarettes. It offended them
to watch my awkwardness

and at last I wanted to eat
nothing but God whom I wanted to swallow whole
whom I wanted to receive completely in my mouth
in my small belly. There was never enough room.
All that divinity.
My mouth stuck open for more
and they believed I was gasping for breath
silently screaming in pain.

It's true what they said
averting their eyes in displeasure
a person could die
or live forever with such hunger.

Lyrics from a *lycée*

1. The classroom

This room my students
inhabit as sparrows
inhabit a cold tree
uneasily
craves warmth and more

light. The little we get
in winter sweeps the wall
mornings, lays a pale hand
on the chalkboard, on definitions
of metaphor

on each bent head. A dull flame
hovers briefly, scatters
a transient glow. I hold my breath
and watch the relentless
fading of each new day.

2. The students

I try to imagine
what's under the skin
what lives inside the slim bodies
the perfect skulls
of these lovely ones.

Something is
straining against flesh
clawing aside veins
and tissue
the way a woman buried alive
might claw away the earth.

Something is beating
like a trapped swallow
against those fine ribs.

It may be exquisite
or something so treacherous
when it breaks through
flesh and skin
reveals tentacles and a fanged mouth
they will be torn
open. They will be helpless
as sheep, their tongues dumb
with terror.

I who have urged them
with my burning words
will find no syllable, no cry
of consolation.

3. The teacher

My child I say
addressing a pupil in my class
you must go early to bed
eat wholesome meat and bread
breathe often of the country air
and take time to play.

I'm sounding so much like my mother
who follows me to unfamiliar towns
wanting to feed and clothe me
with her breath. Her presence
fills the doorway
lingers on windowsills
of each new room. She inhabits
a house completely
making it safe
with the tightly woven texture, steel
bonds of her love.

4. The lesson

I lead my philosophy class
into a stone wilderness
to meet King Lear. The wind
gusts violently as we climb the slope.
Vultures circle silently above us.
I take my students by their soft warm hands
in anticipation of the pain
when the king cries out
My God, my God
why have you forsaken me?

In the falling darkness
someone stumbles. We all come home
with bleeding feet.

Character

If God should permit me to grow
old, I'll turn into a bent crone
difficult, completely unlyrical, my limbs uncertain
and so thin a wind might lift me like a feather.

I'll wear a stained shroud of rags
and let my hair hang grey and matted
to my shoulders like an ancient unused wedding veil.
My chain-smoking will be deemed dangerous

unclean. No doubt I'll belch
often. I'll sit motionless
summoning my last thin fragment of attention
to concentrate on God

while they tap their foreheads
wink and motion to me.
My obstinate refusal to eat anything
but dry bread

will drive the saintliest sister raving
mad. I'll never completely stop
speaking, my slow, insistent words
falling like stones

awkward and deadly in their presence.
I will remain convinced of winning
every argument. Will drive the dagger-sharp
point of my conviction

deep into their dull unwilling minds. Carve
the shape of awkward questions
indelibly on white margins
until the day I die.

Pensées

Everything is circumscribed.
The frail body has its constant
limits and the mind beats
and beats and beats
the cruel air earth fire
and water
the way a bird beats
wings against the memory
of sky

* * *

Try to imagine nails
piercing my small inept hand.
Blood obliterating lifelines.
The yellow nicotine stain.

* * *

Desire for what is perfect
is perfection. It leaves nothing
to be desired. Almost
it puts an end to hunger.

II. GOD EXISTS BECAUSE I DESIRE HIM

How to become anonymous

I dream often of meeting Lawrence
in Aqaba or somewhere on the edge
of the desert. He isn't really dead
only lost in the crowd
and any minute now his cobalt eyes
his sun-burnt face
will float toward me out of the white shroud
rumour has wrapped him in.

We sit quietly in a small cafe
overlooking the gulf
and watch battleships
ghostlike in grey water.
Remembering all wars, Lawrence
speaks lucidly of wounds,
gashes inflicted or received.
He never spares me
ugliness or truth.

How surely his serene words rise,
white pillars no wind-blown sand
or raging ocean can erode.
He teaches me the fearful pleasure
of killing and being killed.
How to vanish: slip quietly
across the drifting bone-white sand
leaving no footprints.

Defence

1.
They said because I wouldn't open my legs
or give my body for pleasure
I wasn't loved by men. They were wrong.
I was kissed in Barcelona
by a Spanish coal-trimmer and once
a man reached out his arms to me.

When I led the march of miners, singing
holding my scarlet flag high
they labelled me *Red*
Virgin of the Tribe of Levi.
Couldn't they tell
these coal-grey, coughing miners
were one with me
and this was love?

        I was adored
by legions of forgotten men
who remember me forever
with tears.

2.
I knew a priest
who knew my heart completely.
Who reached out to me
pure spirit
and touched my soul everywhere
with the flaming point of his love.

3.
Why should anyone be bothered
that as a child I cried out Water, water
I want to wash
when a good friend of the family
leaned over me and kissed
my small soft hand?

On vacation

1.
After exams I came to the countryside and spent ten hours a day rain or sun digging potatoes. The wet smell of earth lodged in my nostrils, my thin back bent like a delicate spring, my arms ached with the weight of potatoes. The greatest heaviness came when they told me in Shanghai striking workers were being shot. This gunfire triggered shocks of anguish in my brain and the fallen bodies weighed on me as I worked. Why wasn't the whole world weeping? Does the gravity of human grief diminish like the law of gravity with distance? Shall we make this the substance of mathematical equations?

2.
In the weeks of wheat harvest I carried sheaves bigger than my own body, lifted them like gold trophies high over my head. They told me this work was for men with prongs but I wouldn't listen. I gathered armfuls of thistles the reapers had separated from the wheat and cradled them defiantly in my bare arms with joy.

3.
On the chill coast of Normandy I covered my head with a large dark hood and when I peered out from it through thick glasses everyone took me for a wolf. I knew then the lean hunger and loneliness of wolves and howled silently inside myself for God who is a kind of wolf and knows the emptiness of an endless night spent stalking.

At last three fishermen welcomed me on board their boat and when they had flung the net spreading it wide over the water I leapt like a glad fish into the cold ocean and held the waves in my slippery arms. We filled baskets with fish and at night I traced star-patterns in the empty sky. No storm had power to alarm me. I stepped out of it dripping like a dog panting with happiness and fierce hunger.

Making the rate
(factory journals)

1.
Mornings I carve washers from bars of sheet metal at the large press and drill a million or so holes in the heavy baffle plate.

Unless you maintain uninterrupted tempo they tell me you won't make the rate. While cutting pieces out of brass strips at the heavy press I botch fourteen. Leon claims the holes aren't centred right and consequently I fail to make the rate.

In the afternoon at a machine operated with buttons I camber the pieces cut this morning, polish one thousand and eight parts at the stamping machine. No one tells me that unless you apply just the right pressure the pulley turns traitor and shifts and the belligerent belt rides off.

Once again I fail to make the rate.

2.
At the end of the morning a machine flails its raging limbs and with bare teeth tears a clump of hair completely from the head of a woman operating it.

In the afternoon the woman is back with a new hairnet. Hard not to stare at the naked spot, a round pale shining, and everyone labours to avoid her. She oils the snarling maniac machine, offers it complete attention and by evening succeeds in exceeding the rate.

3.

It's always a man sets up the press for a woman. The bastards believe they are masters of mechanical performance, know how hard to thrust, just when to bear down, hold back, the right timing and tempo. Their voices when they speak to you are hard as steel. Demands they make about position and control are beyond reason, beyond decency. In the heat of the furnace your arms and thighs drip with sweat. Your heart is a desperate hammer pounding in a hollow room.

4.
While considering Trotsky who never in his life stepped inside a factory I become careless and as a result a small tooth breaks from the saw. This is noticed by the foreman who informs the timekeeper who enters figures on a chart.

Marx and God are problems best abandoned when you're trying desperately to make the rate.

5.
Nenette's friend makes love to a painter morning noon and night. She hints at getting paid and analyzes gladly his techniques in detail for anyone who asks. Evidently she's deprived of nothing and spends her spare time cooking and eating.

Mimi whose sister owns a house in the suburbs tells jokes that would make a regiment of Hussars blush.

The Italian woman is ill and Mouquet has refused leave.

Eugenie says a collection will be taken for Madame Forestier. Josephine and the redhead vow they will give nothing. Nenette and the Italian woman refuse too.

Nenette weeps over coffee, speaking with love of her son who is clever and likes to read. She swears she'll shelter him with her exhausted body, save him with her hungry years from martyrdom and workshops. Tears flood her eyes, her work-worn hands are steel-tight fists.

In spite of the anger smouldering behind half-lowered eyelids, words boiling over, it's cold in the cloakroom where we huddle in our brief, uneasy sisterhood. I bite my tongue to keep from speaking. If I had tears they would fall warm for Nenette.

6.
Today I achieve a rapid cadence which leads to an acceptable tempo which I sustain for several hours and I make the rate and know for a moment standing close to the drilling press a delirious fraternity. A kind of mechanical joy.

7.
I believe workers if they knew the principles of pulleys and crankshafts, the clear meaning of force and counterforce, if they were taught to master the mathematics of machines, logic of transmission belts, they would be filled with proud joy, infused with such spirit the revolution would flare out like a pasque flower and France would at last be free.

Toward evening the clumsy nitwit setting my machine catches his left thumb in a clamp. The bastard bawls out like an ox. His blood drips random patterns on the sea of perfect washers I have polished.

8.
When I count them the round pieces the machine has pressed out slip through my fumbling fingers forcing me to begin again. I can never be sure the final tally is true and what I take home in my pocket in pay determines my true worth as a worker.

I who draw intricate analogies between mathematics and Christ, mediator between the world and God, am lost in the sheer number of metal pieces either perfect or spoiled. My misery is absolute. I bring it home with me daily: a shrill buzzing in my head and a deep aching that will not let me sleep.

9.
At the end of the day I come to the Seine River where I sit exhausted on a stone wall. The silent water as I watch it speaks an invitation so dark and urgent my numb body and my lacerated spirit want to say *yes yes.*

In the nick of time, remembering the foreman, I order my unwilling feet to move and march me quickly across the bridge.

10.
When the bus stops for me and the driver lets me board I'm amazed knowing I've been made a slave and like all slaves have no place anywhere. The whole way I wait for the voice that will order me off. The rough shove of an arm.

At night I lie sleepless on the hard floor and weep for the kindness of the driver.

And if I sleep I dream: machines whining, clanking steel on steel, the hollow thud of the large press grinding piece after piece of humiliation from strips of brass copper tin. The compressed air drill clamps me to its breast and we become one body, the incessant vibration as we dance alien to the soul's rhythm.

A giant hammer beating in my brain.

12.
For once I succeed in replacing free thought with bitterness. The energy thus generated drives me to achieve unusual speed. No spoiled pieces and when I make the rate Leon has nothing to say.

13.
I daydream all day at the machine not bothering to return tools. Botched pieces are concealed, the final tally fabricated. Lunchtime I eat my fill of bread and sausage, drink glass after glass of red wine and offer hand-rolled cigarettes, my last, to Mimi and Nenette.

Pilgims of the absolute

George Orwell took the road to Wigan where he let them lower him body and soul into the earth's black belly. He crawled like a baby on hands and knees, breathed coal dust, learned to keep his head low. His light burning. He spoke when he surfaced earnestly about the collapse of words. When had they become so slovenly, unfit for anything but foolishness? Grief left him mute. Inconsolable. William Carlos Williams climbed up and down tenement steps in the ghetto in north New Jersey learning the open language of sores, syntax of wounds, the imperative mood of desperate wanting. He touched and tongued pain, murmured it home, held it in his mouth while he dreamt. James Agee travelled to Alabama where he entered broken shacks, stepped over thresholds of the bleak, sun-scorched lives of sharecroppers whose constant hunger, unspeakable thirst entered the very marrow of his bones. Whose terrible eyes branded a grammar in his brain fierce as the burning of a factory furnace.

(This is a story about putting on sturdy shoes, travelling light across dark borders. In Paris I practised carrying a single loaf of bread and one ink bottle in the pocket of my only overcoat. After an endless shift in the factory I laboured home, emptied my head of words and slept fitfully on the hard floor.

It is about imagination. Philoctetes, wounded and disarmed, staring with incredible despair, speechless, into his empty hands.)

Credo

Waiting in Saint Etienne
in the *café*, chain smoking,
sharing my hand-rolled cigarettes
with the unemployed I can not speak
of hope.

But I tell them my joy
when God came to me
once in the attic where I slept
bringing me bread and wine.

I believe it is folly
to resolve fear
or close the infinite distance between ourselves
and God
with consolation.

It is also impossible.

Between the sun's rising
and the flaming orange sky of sunset
is wedged the necessary
mystery of affliction and each night
is the season for hunger.

How body and the spirit ache
to consider a child
in China
nursing its bruised bare feet,
its thin hands
stretched out helplessly for rice.

(I imagined God walking
that long distance on wounded feet
balancing bread and wine in his torn hands
and singing. When he rose and left me
I was desolate)

Jew
(definition – a Jew is a person with three or more
 Jewish grandparents)

It wasn't fear made me refuse
absolutely to let anyone accuse me
of Jewishness. I don't deny my one grandfather
sometimes entered the synagogue
and one grandmother may have
kept a kosher kitchen.
Does that make me a Jew?
At home we spread cured ham on bread,
read Pascal and Racine.
My parents were freethinkers and my own thoughts soared
everywhere like eagles.
I knew Hitler was the antithesis of the absolute
good, I said so in my essays.
The stench of burnt flesh blew at me in every shift of wind
until all France became contaminated.

But it wasn't fear. I probed
incessantly the raw sword-edge of truth
and laid it open.

Let no one say I betrayed Jaweh.
How could anyone claim the murderous God
who commanded armies to slaughter
his own warm creation
fathered Jesus who was betrayed, nailed
innocent to a Roman cross?

I was not a fanatic
betrayer. I was betrayed
by their cruel statutes, by their refusal
to let me stand, breathe danger among them,
move my hands, speak out
my burning words. Die. In the end
the sum of my most reasoned logic
served to convince no one
except myself.

Sanctuary

My parents' apartment in Paris became a haven for fugitives. Young workers from Germany slept in their torn clothes on the floor. In the kitchen my mother who refused me nothing made soup for revolutionists who rejoiced believing they'd uncovered at last the Salvation Army.

Trotsky arrived and commandeered the seventh floor. He demanded an extra armchair for his bodyguard who slept with his revolver ready. Trotsky honoured me with insults to my essays, shaved off his moustache, slicked back his thick dark hair and declared himself anonymous.

His family and friends rolled up their coat collars to their noses, pulled felt hats over their eyes and descended together on the service elevator. When it stalled the guard whipped out his black revolver, flourished it with utmost courage over the heads of the masked band that swarmed like an army of beetles into the damp streets of Paris demanding directions of pedestrians: *Which way to the Eiffel Tower? Where can the films of Eisenstein be seen?* Russian oaths, laughter, a trail of broken French leaked muffled through their masks.

All conversations lasted until morning. The fugitives joined in and we agreed on nothing. When Trotsky left we exchanged our last words. They were more courteous than usual, inconclusive, brief. That night I hid them, every syllable, under my pillow.

In Paris

Is it my place
to put on sackcloth
and ashes, a fashion not yet
popular in Paris

or am I the spewed-out
tardy prophet
destined never to arrive
in Tarshish

my credentials water-stained
my terrible duty
to cry out in the city
marketplace

yet forty days

my face burned black
by the east wind
my swollen blood-stained
feet hurtling me headlong

half-crazed
into the sun's cruel blazing.

Revolution

Restless and discontent with being
a spy, I yearned to stand
openly between two soldiers
a loaded gun in my hand. I was impatient
for Spain, for my red scarf,
for my militia uniform. Someone granted me
reluctant permission to select a gun.

At the river crossing my heart beat rapidly with joy.
The sky was sapphire, everything so still
and beautiful. A silver tingling
at my fingertips. I was terrified beyond all
knowing and prepared for wounds.

Someone discovered my clumsiness
and ordered me to a safe place in the camp
cooking. A pot of boiling oil spilled over
on my leg. It wasn't the wound I wanted.

Nor do I want the memory of a boy
captured carrying a picture
of the Blessed Virgin.
Durruti whom I admired in some respects
forced him to choose at fifteen
within a space of the sun's rising
and setting between revolution
and death.

Two anarchists tell me of killing
one prisoner, a priest,
and letting the other go
free. He turned
and when he had walked ten paces
he was shot. At this the anarchists
expected me to laugh.

Interlude

After the Civil War in Spain I turned pacifist
and for a while abandoned politics
for art. In Amsterdam
Rembrandt spoke in sombre tones to the eternal
hunger inside me. I composed poems, dreamed
of rewriting *Electra*, translated the *Iliad*, began
sculpting Justice, her bare unequal arms
holding at uneven levels
equal weights.
I hungered for the absolute
truth of music, beauty of line and colour
the exact texture, pure shape
of love
in the midst of affliction.

Stations

1. Ritual

When the machine had ground me fine
and the heat of the factory furnace
branded me a slave
I came to the Portugal coast. In ghostly moonlight
every hovel in the fishing village wore a gleaming halo.
The sad chant of women circling the small boats
was a prayer so holy it sailed right into my heart
its melodious net stretched
lightly around my aching.

I who had never celebrated
the feast of any saint
understood this
was the religion for slaves and therefore
I would have to stay
until the women finished singing
the candles flickered out
and the only motion was the graceful rocking
of the shadows of the fishing boats
on water.

2. Prayer

In Italy I was a traveller
in homespun and sandals
and like all travellers followed
the sovereign force of converging lines
that drew me with the urgency of thirst
to the unveiled face of Christ.

Mellow fields
cradle the ancient chapel of Santa Maria
in Assissi where I fell for the first time
to my knees.

3. Chant

Holy week in Solesmes a sharp throbbing
pounded the plain sound of Gregorian chant
with the force of hammer blows into my brain.
I abandoned my body
dropping it like an old coat
or a troublesome doubt in a corner
and offered my unburdened spirit
naked to the lyrical and holy
mystery of music

4. Poem

I was reciting a poem about love
I'd learned from an English boy so radiant
he might have been an angel
when Christ descended on me as the swan
descended on Leda.

                    I won't say
I heard the whirring of invisible wings
or felt his touch like breast feathers
but I insist there was a swift tearing
invasion of my spirit.

I was surprised he came from above.

Stepping between the green
hedges of my childhood
I'd imagined God the monster
waiting quietly in the dead centre
of the labyrinth.
After repeatedly arriving
at dead ends
endlessly retracing your steps

you find him at last and he
has nothing to tell you
except himself.

Baptism

I refused to let the priest baptize me although my body longed for the bread he held in his hand and my soul thirsted for wine. Grace and unwavering attention kept me in my rightful place outside the gate where smoke of burning nettles seared my nostrils and the stench of charred flesh satisfied for a while all hunger. Congregations of gaunt eyes, the fellowship of bruised and broken limbs surrounded me.

(Fleeing across the sea to Casablanca we were surrounded by water, blue and holy. If we had been torpedoed we would all have been immersed. A more beautiful baptismal font would not be possible.)

Pensées

Someone is leaping and leaping in the air
each time a little higher. This is not
the way to God. Nor can imagination
fill the emptiness, command growth of wings,
defy gravity.

I am waiting for the utter silence before dawn.
I will not move or weep.
Even desire for grace
may cloud the approaching light
that alone lifts from the heart
all fear.

* * *

From the cross Christ
veiled in the dark
shroud of disbelief
cries out *my God
my God*.

* * *

God exists because I desire him.

III. WE CAN ONLY CRY OUT

Places of abandonment

1.
Travellers *born for felicity*
we grow old
in the Rouen railway station
waiting room. We arrange
and rearrange our faces
holding them closed
tight as the luggage.

We are condemned to wariness
trapped
in the torment of departures
the fear of never ever arriving.
Our worst dreams
the uncertain destinations
of absurd journeys.

I can't escape
the draft from the door
the infernal half-light
weighing down on me.
A death sentence.

I have finished
my last cigarette.
My brain aches.

I am an exile
for whom each train schedule
is the ultimate deception.
I understand at last that while I wait
someone before me barricades
without remorse
the last imagined exit.

2.
My mother and I do not abandon hope
easily, seated on embroidered chairs
beside lace-covered tables
crammed into corners
in *bourgeois parlours full of trinkets
and red plush.*

Pale rays from elegant lamps
illuminate our waiting,
glance from glass ornaments.

We keep coming back
believing
one of the ornate doors will open,
bring to light some government
official, lawyer, the right priest.

We refuse to give up faith
in worn virtues:
patience and importunity.

We refuse food,
all consolation.
We will remain rooted,
growing reproachfully thin.
If need be,
forever.

3.
My imprisoned brother speaks to me
through cast iron grilles
across a distance so great
he is obliged to shout.

We don't speak about the cell
they've locked him in
without paper or pen.
I imagine hell

is like this. Emptiness.
A lack of light.
We cry back
and forth to each other

about mathematics. I remind him
in fractured Greek
God
is the perpetual Geometer.

The guard warns me
foreign languages are forbidden here.
My brother who is brilliant
has factored the concrete equations of fear.

He masters the whole algebra of farewell.

Letters to Antonio, 1940

1.
Because this isn't the time, Antonio,
to speak of love
let me tell you instead of the stars
I'm learning by heart. Evenings
under a clear sky imagine me
a possible shadow
clinging to rock or the damp ground
like the Babylonian shepherds
(no maps, no charts)
putting an end to my ignorance of star-shapes,
names of constellations.

The silence here is vast, more beautiful than music.
Imagine it broken
by a multitude of glittering explosions in the sky
and by the pin-point glow
at the tip of my cigarette.

Are the stars in Africa brilliant? Or soft as distant gunfire?
Does the silence glide immense and luminous and knife-like
into your soul?
I give you all the galaxies, each constellation
except Orion. He is mine.
I'm tearing the stars from his belt and his raised club
for light. I've wrapped the mystery of his lion skin
around my thin shoulders.

2.
The house I live in stands at the edge
of a wood away from the village.
Evenings I build a fire, sweep cobwebs
and dust from the corners
and sleep in a bed of pine needles
scattered on the beaten ground.
Mornings the delicate sound of a finch
singing saves me from the terrible outcry
of the dying. Radiant sky
fills my window.

There is room for you, Antonio, here
beside the small fire on the pine-strewn beaten ground.
But I can't let you come.
We will all live in caves, separated,
away from the light until we are pure enough
for warm houses, nights empty of gunfire.
Until we can walk in the woods
without believing each green tree a cross.

I'm sorry they've taken from you
hills and the ocean.
As long as they've left you the sky
I have the dangerous consolation
of imagining you sheltered:
a blue roof over your head.

3.
I am purified daily
through hard labour in the grape harvest.
I begin by reciting Our Father
in Greek, giving the luminous words
my complete attention. A single stray thought
and I begin again.
Once or twice I have succeeded
in completing the prayer.

By afternoon I can no longer stand upright
in the vineyard. I cut grapes flat on my back,
my sore arms lifted,
the sky a blue flame above me.
I know that God exists:
he has given me the severe mercy
of affliction. Please write and tell me
he is less kind to you.

4.
Believe when I tell you my desire
to set you free. Free as the larks
blood and the heart remember
singing in Spain
mist curled mornings like a shroud
around cold slopes of the Pyrenees.

I was not born for freedom.
I am desperate to exchange places
with you. If this should prove impossible
we are both lost.

I'm watching the sun set on the Mediterranean,
the blinding light, the beauty, unbearable.
Unless beauty and light should hold enough
grace to destroy distance,
tear out barb-wire walls and burn them
to ash
setting the chained body
the charged mind
free.

5.
When you get this letter
I will be gone. I am leaving home
a boat is waiting.
You will not hear from me often

distance being what it is,
war, the laceration
of departures
and everything else contrary

to truth. My last gifts to you
are these: a poem, clothing for a cold night
a little money, names whose melody
may comfort you. Forgive me.

And thank you for your tender words, Antonio,
describing the ocean. When at last it holds me
in its infinite sorrow
I may think of you. The wind

blowing wherever it desires
will occasionally unite us
(I pray to God)
in our divided thoughts.

Exile

1.
In the refugee camp at Casablanca
we wrap ourselves in coarse blankets
and sleep seventeen nights on the ground.

I imagine myself a pilgrim in the desert
travelling like Lawrence on a camel
and pitching my tent nightly under cold stars

on the sand. Several hundred Jews around me
dream of New York. It is the stone oasis
they all long for. Mornings the breeze

blows from the Atlantic
while Polish rabbis faithfully chant prayers
in a nearby garden. My parents

as if preparing me for America
or a great sacrifice, hover over me
with outspread wings. They always save me

one of the few camp chairs to sit on
and urge me to eat. Thoughts of God
pour out like blood

through every nerve and fibre,
through fingertips, pen, ink, into my notebook
and I am busy until our ship leaves

for New York. (A city difficult to circumvent
on this pilgrimage. The sooner I arrive in port
the sooner I can leave.)

2.
Everyone on board danced
when we passed Bermuda. Nights warm.
Laughter and wine. I

stood alone on deck
wind and sea spray cold on my face.
Ocean and sky black.

If I should cry out now
who would hear me?

3.
Waiting for shore. The end
of headaches.
A thin measure of light.

4.
From New York I send clandestine letters
to friends in different wildernesses
begging them for aid in my escape.

Locked in my room in silence
I experience a hunger so deep
nothing can be done for it.

Mornings I attend mass, Sundays
join believers in the Baptist church
in Harlem. I behold such joy

in worship, I want to fling my thin body
into the dancing, lift my empty arms
to God

      whom I beg in mercy
to make me a paralytic, witless,
mute as a stone and blind. I long to be

consumed completely, my imperfect body
transformed, portioned bit by bit
to the afflicted. My nothingness

my imperfect faith by grace
freely
made nourishment

Memos to a government in exile

1.
This is to inform you of my vocation for danger, my undeniable calling to suffering and death. I request your permission, your help and your unfettered blessing. Send me to the front, to the fateful centre of the battle which is my rightful place.

I have asked God to make me a cripple, paralyze my arms, thighs, legs. Immobilize my neck and torso. In return I've pledged him absolute attention.

I beg you to send for me soon.

2.
I dream nightly of leading a small band of women into war where the danger is greatest. Where blood pools from wounds gaping in the dust and sun, and the outcry of the dying consumes the sombre light. Where the night is riddled with machinegun fire and fear. Where only the cold rain washes the stiffening corpses.

We will be faultless as doves, tranquil as angels whose wings hold healing. We will wrap ourselves in the skin of a white lion. We will come singing.

This dream is given to me by God. I have carried it in my arms the way one carries an only child: with hunger and love and constant trembling. It is my duty and my desperate joy to lay it before you.

Tacitus tells us we will not be the first. Germanic tribes, nomads of the first century sent virgins into battle, surrounded them with warriors, the bravest and best. Do you imagine it impossible to find in France women with an equal measure of grace? Women with courage in their clasped hands? Believe me when I tell you we will be ready for death.

(I have warned you we will be few. And as I promised, undefiled.)

3.
When we have buried the last dead, scrubbed their blood from our hands, the caked mud and tears from our faces, what then? Then we must believe God, for whom the heart longs, exists a great distance beyond everything we have imagined. Beyond the stars, beyond the expanding universe. Beyond thought. The desire to reach him is a great folly.

We must abandon hope. Turn our backs on consolation.

We can only cry out.

Pensées

Beauty and affliction are one. A white rose
rain-blessed and pure prompts *why*
briefly. But pain's bewildered *why*
why why
has no end except silence.

Listen.   Listen.

* * *

Hunkered in the ashes, Job
scrapes his ulcerated arms, chest,
with shards of memory, splinters of lost joy.
Friends gather like flies around affliction.
Their brittle words wound deeper than shards,
shatter the redeeming silence.

He tries to remember the road
travelled to get this far,
gathers his desolation like a worn dark
cloak around his shoulders,
listens to the incandescent moon. The sea.
Hears himself, surprised, cry out: *I know
that my redeemer lives.*

* * *

Affliction is nothing
in itself. The laceration of the mind
merely, a slit, a sculpture in the flesh
forgotten when the pain goes.

It is nothing
until it completes in silence
the shape and texture that is Christ's
unspeakable suffering.

Colour

Sometimes when a cruel migraine
turned the world black, when war came
closer, I was considered dangerous
my longing for that dark and silent childhood
mountain believed unreasonable
my inordinate hunger for danger
improper. The colour of the gospel
I wanted to proclaim

had everybody worried. (Even de Gaulle
cleared off a corner desk in a dark room
commanding me to write my mad and vivid dreams
to the last detail on a white page.)

I'd like to tell you I was born a child of light
a creature with transparent wings
that lifted me until a winter moon shone
as if through gossamer
all green and gold and shimmering.

Truth is
in spite of the drab leather of my shoes
my worn grey overcoat, my winter skin
I was the colour of fire.

Centre

In London I lived in a tiny room at the top
and through my window I could see
trees with branches full of sparrows.
Looking straight up at night
I beheld the silence of a black heaven
seeded with stars.

I dreamt in that room of climbing a steep path
of coming closer to the sun
or to some destination I'd been walking all my life
toward. The air
uncluttered here caressed me
like a silk feather. And I knew
I was near that dangerous centre
that when I arrived would explode
everything would cease and I would finally be
nothing.

If there is truth it would then be visible.
It would be infinitely good.

London, 1943

Spring was exquisite that year.
Air shimmering with birdsong curfew couldn't silence.
Woodbine and fireweed weaving a green shroud
around bomb rubble. The city's wounds
wrapped in unrationed perfume: apple blossom,
lilac so sweet it snatched your breath away.

From behind smashed walls and windowless houses
the summer voices of children drifted.
An infinite silvery dream
spun out past evening blackout,
warm as June rain washing the stubborn dust
from every crevice in the broken street.

Letter to a friend

I've taken a London landlady for my mother.
Those lean boys loitering in bomb rubble
stuffing their pockets with stones
are my brothers.

I have a sister too.
Mornings she changes the blood-stained sheets,
scrubs the bars of my bed
all the while singing love songs
in her English country voice.

Letters I've given the ocean for my parents
in America, will bring news
however incomplete.

I'm still looking for a father
and a country to call me home.

Until then I remain
sleepless in my clean bed while my sister sings
for me and my vagrant brothers
grow thin as reeds in the bitter street.

The landlady when she steps inside
these four white walls must remain
always my loving mother. Always
hungry.

Morning

I'm surprised how much of the world is mine.
The unbearable volume of loveliness:
frail evening light, the way the east wind shivers
the willow tree. I own all birdsong
lodged beneath my ribs' fragility. The stones too
and the stars

a million shapes and silences.
They find unerringly the body's furthest crevice
the way December snow sifts through
slits in a broken building.

I've received the wind's burning
laceration, lies,
the voices gunfire couldn't silence.

Thirty-three years.

You see how carefully I carry them
in my awkward arms.
Faces of Mother and Father remain
familiar as the spring-shade of Paris,
texture of new vines, mist
veiling the river.

From my bed this morning I can see
the whole sky, a scarlet flame.
Its light is terrible beyond words
and holy. Shivering like an autumn willow leaf
I must behold it
knowing everything it means.

Love Song

I've begged them to fly me somewhere
toward home
which is enemy territory
parachute me like the seed of a dandelion
into a field or forest
in France where I'll take root
and when the first green shoot of me pushes
pure as a lily through the earth's brown skin, visible
evidence of my true love
and spring's miraculous returning,
the enemy will lose heart, turn
noiseless as the ebbing tide
and everyone will finally rejoice.

Do this, I plead, before my flesh withers
completely and my blood runs dry.
I am the kind who die young, who die
grappling toward sunlight. Trapped
in this alien country, fog always in my throat
I've had enough of waiting, enough
of words.
Like Icarus and Leonardo I ask for nothing
but wings.

Still hungry

though I've swallowed more than I can hold
of fear. Not fear
a dagger will split open the heart
breath cease
the enemy lay a siege so brutal
there's no healing for the wounded.

Have I said how butterflies crumble
and fade when a child's hand
caresses their submissive wings
how the brown and gold dust clings
with the force of hunger to the skin?

Nothing I know can brush away
the horror of that fading.
Of that tenacious dust.

Grief

They've brought me broken beyond mending
into a room silent and pure as a mountain
I remember from childhood. Here
they offer me a cup of eggwhite whipped with sherry
and a very ripe peach.

They believe I'm dying of hunger, not knowing
hunger is the kind of grief leaves you sterile
as stone
in which no seed can germinate.
Sorrow enters you and you become
the colour of dead leaves.

The greatest grief is knowing what I hold
inside my throbbing head,
what I hunger to offer the world
remains invisible to their blinded eyes.
I want to cry out in rage, force them to probe
each lucent phrase I've spoken, rip open
every syllable, eat every word. Why don't they
seize me violently by my frail shoulders,
grasp my transparent hand in theirs and ask:
Are these things true?

Room

I entreated them to bring me closer to the coast
a place with leafy trees and a wide green meadow
where I imagined the sea breathing
on a veiled shore. Where the delicate outline of France
is visible to the mind's eye and the sky
spreads, a blue shield from horizon to horizon.
Where the wind sings.

I was a citizen of big cities,
had breathed the acrid air in factories,
marched in dark streets
and wept for the whole world.

Waiting is the necessary prelude to truth
but I could wait no longer to leave
London behind me.

No earthly country, no room,
only the universe is vast and beautiful enough
to die in.

Outside the gate

It wasn't despair or fear
not lack of nourishment nor lack of consolation.
Something I had unwillingly foreseen
crept up from each extremity
a cold tide inching toward the heart.

August warming the somber meadow grass,
these old stones. This morning
someone plucked roses from a London garden
bound them in colours of France
cradled them the whole distance with love
and laid them rootless on the broken ground.
Look how the petals wilt. (Under the sun
will some seed fall like wheat into the fertile earth?)

I was always far from home
uneasily rooted, outside the city limits
where I belonged, outside the gate
the fabricated wall only the singing birds
night bombers
and flaming thoughts fly over.

Why do they weep?
They will learn how I fed on light
and became fire. And yet

if there were strength in this ill-cut body
voice to whisper
I would beg like the foolish king, driven into wilderness
and mad (no mother, father
no daughter to press a flower in his stiffening hand):
Pray you undo this button.

Dirge

What's left is the impenetrable
cloud of unknowing
and the implicit stars. Mystery
not importunity will keep their sharp points veiled.
Larks warble. The beloved wind
blowing where it chooses
shreds clouds into the myriad
fragments of regret. Is it desire
stirs morning grass into an emerald sea?

                Who's there to tell us
the afflicted (if attentive
and motionless and mute)
will catch above time's cruel transience
above the swallow's flight
an echo of the absolute? The unmistakable
breath-taking wingbeat of grace.

The author is indebted to the following sources:

Jacques Cabaud, *Simone Weil: A Fellowship in Love* (New York: Channel Press, 1964)

Robert Coles, *Simone Weil: A Modern Pilgrimage* (Reading, Massachusetts: Addison Wesley Publishing Company, Inc, 1987)

Gabrielli Fiori, *Simone Weil*, tranlated by Joseph R. Berrigan (Athens, Georgia: The University of Georgia Press, 1989)

Simone Petremont, *Simone Weil: A Life* (New York: Pantheon Books, 1976)

Simone Weil, *Formative Writings, 1929-1941*, edited and translated by Dorothy Tuck McFarland and Wilhelmine Van Ness (Amherst: University of Massachusetts Press, 1987)

The Simone Weil Reader, edited by George A. Panichas (New York: David McKay Company, Inc., 1977)

Simone Weil, *Gravity and Grace*, with an introduction by Gustave Thibon (New York: Octagon Books, 1981)

Simone Weil, *Gateway to God*, edited by David Raper with the collaboration of Malcolm Muggeridge and Vernon Sproxton (Collins Fontana Books, 1974)

Other books by Sarah Klassen:

Journey to Yalta (Turnstone Press, 1988)

Violence and Mercy (Netherlandic Press, 1991)

Borderwatch (Netherlandic Press, 1993)

Dangerous Elements (Quarry Press, 1998)